All Our Wandering
Vol 1

ABOUT THE AUTHOR

Daithi Neavyn is a writer rooted in the landscapes of Ireland but whose life also stretches to Guatemala, a place that feeds his curiosity and creativity. Though his years of exploration have mellowed, his fascination with the world's diversity and beauty remains as bright as ever.

Daithi finds inspiration in the natural world, weaving reflections on belonging, culture, and spirit into his work. A background in permaculture and Shamanic studies, alongside founding Nomad Yurts, reflects his lifelong commitment to sustainable, grounded ways of living.

Now, much of his energy flows into writing. In *The House of Oaks and Owls*, his weekly Substack, Daithi explores themes of home, nature, and the quiet revelations that come from looking inward and outward at once. He writes with a heart anchored in Ireland, always watching the horizon for what might come next.

All Our Wondering Vol 1 is his first publication.

All Our Wandering Vol 1

Daithi Neavyn

Self-Published: Daithi Neavyn

Email: daithineavyn@gmail.com

First Edition 2024

Copyright © 2024 by Daithi Neavyn

All rights reserved. No part of this publication may be reproduced, stored in a retrieval system, or transmitted in any form or by any means, electronic, mechanical, photocopying, recording, or otherwise, without prior written permission from the author, except for brief quotations in reviews or articles.

Cover Design by Daithi Neavyn

This is a work of nonfiction. However, in order to respect privacy and maintain confidentiality, the names of certain individuals and identifying details have been changed.

ISBN: 9798303721425

For permissions, inquiries, or additional information, please contact:

daithineavyn@gmail.com

Acknowledgement

I would like to express my deep gratitude to Karuna Atitlán, where the supportive environment and shared passion for storytelling helped shape this project, and to Luke Maguire Armstrong for his invaluable mentorship and encouragement throughout the creation

@authorlukema

@karunaatitlan

To my Mum and Dad,
who gifted me the love of reading,
the magic of words,
and an eye for the finer things in life.

"We shall not cease from exploration, and the end of all our exploring will be to arrive where we started and know the place for the first time."
— T.S. Eliot

All Our Wandering
Volume 1

Table of Contents

ABOUT THE AUTHOR i

Acknowledgement iv

Table of Contents i

PROLOGUE 1

LA CUEVA 4

THE GARDENER OF THE ALHAMBRA 12

AFTERNOON TEA WITH MEN 19

WHERE THE FIRES LEAD 44

THE HEART OF BRIGHTNESS 54

THE GOLDEN AGE 60

HIMALAYAN DREAMING 69

THE FOX..77

Between Here and There: 81

PROLOGUE

Nomadic Echoes

Sneha G Gupta, CC BY-SA 4.0 'Footprint on the ground' via Wikimedia Commons

I once met a man who stepped outside his back door and fell into wonder. And others, I've learned, stepped out long ago and are still trying to find their way home. In each of us, the ghost of a nomadic ancestor echoes through time.

Picture a hunter. He bends to touch the tracks of an animal he is following. Meltwater flows past his feet, and as he cups it in his hands to drink, he watches the snowline retreat across the distant mountains. Everything around him is home. No thought of being elsewhere stirs in his mind. As sure as an arrow finding its mark, he rises each day with quiet readiness to meet his world.

Two forces shape his life: depth and expansion. Depth calls him to be still, to submerge himself in the full presence of place. Expansion, its counterbalance, sends him outward, exploring new trails, new horizons. Together, they create a rhythm. Today, we mistake expansion for rootlessness—skipping across capitals, hopping continents. But true nomadic living is nothing of the sort. Nomadic people are always moving, but they are never uprooted. To them, the land is home, no matter where their journey takes them. They are grounded, carrying their connection with them.

Being of a place is a rare and beautiful thing. Every traveler, whether knowingly or not, seeks encounters with those who embody it. We sense their fierce bond with the land, and we long for it too. In their eyes, we glimpse our own wandering soul and feel the ache of disconnection. Something in us keeps open this door of longing, echoing the absence we carry, like the earth releasing a sweet exhale at dawn.

There is alchemy in the act of traveling—a setting out and a returning. Every true journey moves both outward and inward, uncovering forgotten places within ourselves. Sometimes, a journey leads us to fall in love again—with wonder, with the reawakening of places inside us we thought had faded long ago. And yet, there they are, rising like the first green shoots breaking through spring soil.

This book is a collection of such moments. It tells of encounters with people who carry the essence of place, of journeys that brought clarity, and of moments when I rediscovered home, both in the world and myself. Travel has taught me that the world still holds hidden corners waiting to be noticed and that, when we stop to listen, the quiet song of water, wind, and earth can heal us.

LA CUEVA

Las Alpujarras, Spain

Muffinn from Worcester, UK, 'Spanish Mountains' CC BY 2.0 via Wikimedia Commons

Below me, a valley drops steeply into shadow, and the soft sound of water rises from below. My only thought is to arrive, anchoring me to the path. I drop my backpack to the ground again and slump against a stone wall on the forest path. My breath billows in cold plumes, marking the frigid air. A map, crumpled and worn, is in my right hand, looking as tired as I feel.

Ah, yes, my map. If this journey were a comedy, the map would be the punchline. An acquaintance sketched it hastily with a stub of a pencil—a snaking line, a sendero crossing two valleys and striking north across the page. Somewhere in those two inches of pencil line, here I am. This slip of paper, this incompetent companion that demands more information than it gives, has already cost me painful extra hours. But I cling to it still. When he handed the map to me, my friend tapped twice on the village marked as Capileira. "Go there," he said. "Meet Miguel in La Cueva. It's a special place." Those words cast a spell. That spell is what keeps me going, the thought of finally arriving and pushing open the doors of La Cueva.

A sound brings me back, and I see a shepherd's dog bounding out of the forest onto the track. He runs toward me, a mass of white and golden-brown fur swaying. He skids to a stop, looks me over and disappears into the trees behind me. A flock of goats come into view, bells dangling from their necks, and a man behind them. He moves slowly, his right hand clutching a walking stick which he uses to pull himself up the path, defying gravity. He calls out to his animals in a guttural Alpujaran accent.

I stand up as he approaches. Embarrassed, I hand him the rudimentary slip of paper I call a map. "Voy a Capileira," I tell him, pointing to the spot on my map. He takes it, raising it close to his eyes. He considers my question and smiles, and I sense he understands: he sees in a flash my exhaustion and eagerness to be off the trail. "Dos horas," he says. He points up the track I must follow, then crouches down to drink from the stream at our feet. When he rises up again, he folds the map neatly and places it in my palms. There's a lightness in his eyes that might be mistaken for simplicity but in this one gesture he helps diffuse my frustration with the map.

How our plans can be derailed by those things we encounter on our path. Frustration for one. The shepherd continues on through the forest, following a path he has probably walked since childhood, and leaves me with a gift he may not even realise.

I place the map in my pocket and continue on. This morning began in a dazzle of brightness and ambition. My plan was simple: reach Capileira, find La Cueva, and drink wine after the day's walk. I moved along, light as a stream. Early arrival seemed possible, and I felt giddy with optimism, buoyed by the sun and the breeze. I pictured my arrival, imagined conversations filling my mind.

They'll ask, 'Where are you going?' and I'll say, 'La Cueva'—as if that's all they need to know.

Now, in the late afternoon, with fading light and increasing hunger, I've reached the point where I just want to arrive. The sweet, playful youth of the morning has long gone. Even the beautiful vistas—a hare darting across a field, a hawk overhead—feel lifeless to me now. "Come on," I tell myself, summoning an image of Arctic explorers trekking through icy streams on little more than three biscuits. "Come on," I say, steeling for the last stretch.

My steps are a slow prayer. The path zigzags upward, and I reach a ridge at the edge of an open field. I can see the peak of a mountain in the Sierras, capped with a light dusting of snow. In the valley, a line of mulberry trees catches the last sunlight on their dark green leaves. It was rich history of this land that brought me here, and the mulberry tree stands out as a potent symbol of past times. The Arabs carved this land to their will; they crafted irrigation channels to replenish their crops, and above all else the mulberry tree played an essential role in their economy, lifestyle, and agriculture. All those hours of labour I thought to myself, the sweat and exhaustion that went into working this land. I let that thought sit with me, with the sweat on my own brow in this place rich in history. "Two hours," the shepherd said. I look into the sky; the light is fading now, the forest growing quiet.

Another hour of walking passes before I finally see it—the most beautiful sight for a weary traveler—the last sign for my destination: Capileira. I stand before it and reach out to touch it as though I don't trust it is there. Exhaustion is my companion now, for what arrival is not magnified by a strenuous journey? I catch my first sight of Capileira and walk the final steps into the edges of the village. The street squeezes between white-painted houses, with faint light glowing behind shutters. I keep walking as my footsteps echo on the stones and enter a small plaza, where a mature tree commands the center, and I know I've arrived.

La Cueva is there before me and it is stirring to life. From outside, I see the silhouette of the owner; a man I'd come to know as Miguel, moving between tables with the grace of a matador, shaking out tablecloths and arranging the cutlery. He lights candles, one on each table and across the bar top. A warm glow fills the inside. The piano receives special attention: he brushes dust from its stool and carefully positions it, poised for the first notes. When all is set, he takes a bottle of wine, pours himself a small glass, studies the wine, and drinks with a flick of his wrist.

I cross the street and step inside. A few customers are already seated, but Miguel calls out a warm welcome, waving me in. La Cueva is indeed cave-like in the dark embrace of its interior. Dark wood frames the walls, ceiling, and floor, creating the sense of a forest within. A waft of sweet pine wood fills the air. I move along the perimeter, taking it all in. The mosaic of pictures and artifacts—adventures, ancestry, erotica, and remnants of the Golden Age—draws my eye to walls dripping with memory. Marilyn Monroe's gaze meets mine, her image claiming space beside a black-and-white photograph of a football team and their stadium. Eva Peron, wrapped in a white scarf, stands proudly beside a row of iron skillets, each long handle nailed above a black stove. I reach out and push one, and it swings back like an old creaking pendulum. Further on, in a recess dimly lit by a single bulb, bullfighting posters blazoned in reds and oranges jostle for room, peeling away like forgotten memories. I move to an area filled with family photos: grandparents hand in hand, children dressed in their best, generations captured and displayed, each face a reminder of time passing.

"Vino de Cantabria!" someone shouts, and I turn to see a large Spanish man enter. He swings his heavy brown jacket off his shoulder and drags it across the floor. His face glows with joy, and he hangs his brown suede hat on a hook. "Ah, Francesco!" Miguel greets him warmly. "Claro, claro, Cantabria!" The two embrace. "Hay música esta noche?" Francesco asks with a grin. Miguel looks mock-surprised. "Siempre!" he says, and they both laugh.

People are arriving now, and La Cueva fills with conversation, laughter, and warmth. Miguel, noticing I am still standing, comes over and guides me to a seat with a gentle hand on my elbow. My eye is drawn to a painting on the wall. It's a portrait of a young girl in a white dress, her innocent smile framed by carved wood more ornate than any other frame. Curious, I ask Miguel who she is.

"Martha, my father's sister," he says, his voice soft. "Beautiful, isn't she? She was the youngest." He continues, "My grandfather had a farm nearby, with terraced walls and fruit trees. But…" His voice falters. "The war years were hard. Martha caught pneumonia at seven. She didn't survive."

We look at the portrait in silence. Martha's gaze seems to hold all the lightness of a childhood cut short. "I look at that painting every day," Miguel says quietly before returning to his hosting.

La Cueva is lively, yet holds an intimacy that invites you to slow down and savor the moment. After my long day of walking, the warmth, food, wine, and company are a balm. As the night progresses, Miguel raises his glass, calling for silence. "¡Música!" he declares, to a round of approving cheers, and gestures to a young woman at the piano. Francesco leans back in his chair, smiling broadly. Everyone listens as the first notes rise; many close their eyes, sighing with pleasure.

The music unfolds its magic in the room. Like a cresting wave, it lifts us forward, cradling us. Miguel catches the chorus, and others join. The piano notes dance, each table united, the singer's voice drawing us together.

I catch sight of Martha's portrait again. Her eyes seem to watch us, as though her spirit is here, joining in our song as the final line is sung, "Y el amor siempre será."

In that moment, La Cueva breathes life into us all. The world outside is left to its own devices—just for tonight. And how big that world is, I think to myself. How many paths there are to follow. I take the map from my pocket one last time, unfolding and folding it again. Under Martha's watchful eyes, I place it in a small recess in the wall.

THE GARDENER OF THE ALHAMBRA

Granada, Spain

Martinvl, CC BY-SA 4.0, 'Alhambra Palace, via Wikimedia Commons

Reclining in the Alhambra courtyard that morning, I yearned for a forgotten world. The calm the Moors had sought to evoke was drowned in modern noise. I lingered, searching for a quieter rhythm, the Andalucian heat pressing down. Around me, tourists bustled—selfie sticks rising like periscopes, voices blending into a chorus of distraction.

I moved between the rooms and sat by a still pool bordered in blue tiles. A gentle trickle of water flowed along a stone channel - the subtlest of music, the quiet song of water. But who could hear it today? I lingered, unwittingly in the background of photos, trying to focus on a quieter place where the Islamic designs, rooted in contemplation, could be felt. The blue sky above was framed by the ornate tiled walls as though reaching towards heaven. A flock of birds blazed across my vision and I decided to go outside.

In time, I wandered to the Generalife, following the Acequia Real to its lush gardens. Beneath towering cypress trees, I found a gravel path, shaded by almond and cherry branches brushing together like whispered secrets. Aromatic herbs grew at my feet; lavender, thyme, and rosemary—their scent rising with each step. Here, at last, I could breathe. I paused by an old stone wall, where lizards slipped between cracks in the dry earth, and loquat and quince trees cast shade over the path. The Chinese say, "All life's problems can be solved in a garden." As I passed through the quieter corners of the Generalife, far from the crowds, my mood began to lighten.

I stepped beneath an archway into a shaded avenue, where jasmine and wisteria twisted together overhead, their fallen blossoms scattered like confetti along the path. A rhythmic snip, snip broke the stillness—the sound of pruning shears at work. Through the wisteria's leafy canopy, I glimpsed a man, his back to me, carefully tending each stem with measured precision.

I paused, leaning lightly against the archway's cool metal frame, watching. After a moment, I stepped closer.

He straightened, sliding his secateurs into a worn leather holster at his side. His movements were unhurried, deliberate, the mark of someone attuned to the task. A broad-brimmed leather hat, faded and sun-creased caught my eye, framing his face as he turned to meet my gaze.

"Not many people come to this part of the garden," he said.

"I was looking for a quiet place away from the crowds," I replied.

He smiled, "Well then, let me show you something." He extended a hand in greeting. "Soy Giorgio."

We walked beneath the shade of cypress trees, their leaves dancing in intricate patterns across the ground. Giorgio moved ahead, his steps light and purposeful, as if each turn of the path were second nature. He veered off the main trail, stepping over a jagged stone outcrop and weaving through dense oleander bushes. I quickened my pace to keep up, curiosity pulling me along.

After a while, Giorgio slowed, coming to a stop. He glanced back at me with a kind smile and gestured to a nearby bench shaded by overhanging branches. "Let's rest here for a moment," he said, settling into the quiet.

As we sat, I asked, "How did you come to work in these gardens, Giorgio?"

He leaned back, his expression softening. "Ah, that story begins after my wife passed," he said, his voice low and steady. "These gardens were her favorite place. At first, I only came to feel close to her, to sense her spirit lingering here. Over time, the place grew on me too. One day, the head gardener noticed me and invited me to help out—a few quiet hours here and there, far from the crowds. I suppose I never left."

The story lingered between us, carried by the rustle of leaves. "So, you live here now?" I asked gently.

"In a way," he replied with a faint smile. "Each morning, I brew my coffee and come out here. The plants tell me what they need. It's a rhythm I've come to cherish." Rising to his feet, he motioned for me to follow. "Let me show you my favorite spot."

We continued along a narrow, winding path, the soft murmur of unseen water accompanying our steps. Giorgio led the way with the quiet confidence of someone deeply rooted to this place. Eventually, we reached an archway draped in thick, twining plants. He passed through the frame without hesitation, as if crossing a threshold into a secret world.

Beyond the arch, the air grew cooler, the sky hidden by an interwoven canopy of leaves. In the center of the clearing stood a small, weathered fountain, surrounded by moss-speckled cobblestones. Giorgio stopped beside it, the serene expression on his face matching the sanctuary's stillness. For a moment, it felt as though time itself had paused.

A cracked stone basin stood at the center, weathered but enduring, its water flowing in a gentle, melodic stream before vanishing into the earth. The soft song of water filled the air, a quiet pulse of ancient Al-Andalus. In its rhythm, there was healing—a tender embrace that seemed to wash over us, carrying whispers of the past.

"People rarely come here," Giorgio said.

"Why not?" I asked.

He paused, then answered simply, "Because most never look."

I lingered, letting the soft murmur of the fountain fill the silence. The weight of past losses seemed to ebb away, replaced by gratitude for what endured. Giorgio moved quietly among the plants, his hands at home in the soil, until he glanced up and said, "The past is always with us. It hides in the earth, in the stone, in the water. You just have to notice."

This secluded corner, with its weathered fountain and quiet song of water, felt like a living poem—one of Giorgio's hidden treasures. For a moment, I imagined I was the first to uncover it in years.

As we stepped back into the sunlight, the cypress trees stretched tall and motionless against the sky.

"How long do you plan to keep working here, Giorgio?" I asked.

He smiled faintly. "Oh, I retired long ago. I just come every day, because the gardens need me—and I suppose I need them." He pressed my hand warmly between his. "It was good to meet you," he said. "But I should get back to my work."

I thanked him and watched as he disappeared down the shaded path, his figure blending into the greenery, as if he were part of the garden itself. It was time for me to leave. Shadows stretched across the forest floor, lengthening with the sun's descent. As I walked back toward the palace, birds took flight, their wings filling the air with motion and song as if echoing the melody of the fountain I'd left behind.

Left alone, I thought about Giorgio again. To the world, he might seem like an old man lost in the past, but here in the Generalife, he was never alone. His wife's spirit lingered in the gardens, and the gardens, in turn, brimmed with life.

I felt the quiet wisdom he had shared settle in: never stop seeking hidden places. Sometimes, if you're fortunate, someone will guide you there.

AFTERNOON TEA WITH MEN

Tabernas Desert, Almeria, Spain

Colin C Wheeler, CC BY-SA 3.0 ES 'Olive Tree' via Wikimedia Commons

They told me to follow the Rambla: "There are a lot of interesting people living out there that you ought to meet." So I followed it straight into the desert of Tabernas in Almería, in the far southeast of Spain. I was a young man then, in my late twenties, full of youthful curiosity, with more questions than answers under my belt. I figured that anyone who chose to live in a place like this might have something interesting to say—maybe even something to teach me.

On a morning with no chance of rain, I walked the Rambla, the name given to the dried-out riverbed; a stretch of flat earth and red ground that winds through the scrub and crumbling desert rocks. The Alhamillas mountains rose in the south, and behind them was the Mediterranean Sea and the coastline of Cabo de Gata.

But I was here for the desert—for the land where Sergio Leone shot his Spaghetti Westerns. Where men on the edge of the law forged their own paths. For better or worse, the mythology of those films was soaked into the landscape.

The first sign of human habitation caught my eye—a blue flag tied to a pole at the entrance to someone's land. Is this Alex's place, I wondered? I was told to meet him first. I entered the enclosure—and that is the right word—passing through a fence made of bamboo canes and metal bars, with a sign painted in fat white letters on old plywood: "Private. No entry." The yard around me looked like a salvage depot, a playground of found objects dragged in from the desert—abandoned projects, discarded structures, an old fridge lying on its side, and most bizarrely, a sack of broken dolls that looked like it had fallen out of a child's worst dream.

Two dogs came charging through the yard towards me, and quick as their bark, a voice called them back. Reluctantly, they retreated. It was a man's voice, high-pitched and erratic but firm. I could hear him rummaging through things out of sight—the sounds of metal banging off metal, and objects being thrown aside. I waited a moment, then he came into view. As he approached, beaming broadly, he thrust a tremendous hand into mine, causing it to tremble as if a jackhammer had come to life.

"I'm Alex," he said, brushing his hands down his jeans. I told him why I was there and where I had come from, and he listened with interest.

"Okay," he said. "You're here now, and your timing is good. I was about to take a break."

Alex invited me into the tented structure he called his home and started to prepare tea. I sat down on the benches by the main table—a heavy lump of wooden planks pinned together and illuminated by a single hanging lightbulb. The kitchen was stocked like a wartime rations store, full of jars and a line of blue plastic drums with words scrawled on their sides. I could see "trigo," which I knew meant flour. There were stacks of books and magazines on the shelves, covering much of the perimeter. The word "survival" in thick black letters stood out on one spine. I felt like an object blown in from the desert that had roused this man's interest.

"Do you know where I'm from?" Alex asked. "I'm one-quarter Romanian Gypsy, one-quarter Native American, one-quarter English, and one-quarter Polish." He pounded the kitchen counter with his palms and leaned back, laughing.

"Yeah, Gypsy, Native American, English, and Polish. My father was a gamekeeper on a big estate in England. I lived with him for a few years, and he used to take me out hunting with him."

Alex sat across from me. His wiry, muscular frame, six feet six inches tall, arched over the space as he swayed back and forth, picking splinters of wood from the table. He was like an old dog with one open eye, and I watched his hands slide along the surface—the fingers like tree roots, the skin dark and tanned.

"What was the family of that estate called?" Alex asked himself, rubbing his chin. "The Underwoods, that was it. Wonderful people, big family; they had seven children. I used to run around the fields with them as a child."

Candlelight flickered off the dark recesses at the back of the tent. Nothing was fully revealed. I strained to see something—there was a faint clicking sound.

Alex continued, "Hah, and then I kissed the youngest daughter, and that was that. I wasn't allowed to play with them anymore."

He threw his head back and laughed. I laughed a little with him. I was beginning to settle into his energy and come around to liking him. This roused the others in the tent.

I returned my gaze to the source of the clicking sound and let my eyes settle there, and then I noticed them—two more people; a man and a woman, I thought, staring into faint computer screens. Neither had spoken yet nor turned to note my presence.

"Debs, where's my gift from the Blackfoot?" Alex called out.

"In the back," she replied without looking away from the screen.

Alex went to the back of the tent. "It's wrapped in some green fabric on one of the boxes," Debs said.

Alex returned to the table with a cloth in his hand. "Okay, here we have it." With ceremonial delicacy, he placed the cloth on the table between us and let it rest there. He reached out, uncurling the edges to reveal a large knife.

"Something else, eh?" Alex said, watching my reaction. Light and shadows flickered across the blade as we stared at it. It looked heavy, like a lump hammer. The blade was cold and about fourteen inches long; the steel was dark grey, turning lighter at the edges. There was a smell of old leather on the handle, and red and black beads on thick threads hung from it.

"It's from the Blackfoot tribe," Alex said.

"It's beautiful," I replied, wondering where all of this was leading.

"Pick it up," Alex said. "But don't touch the edge. It'll cut."

I had hoped for a cup of tea and a chat about life in the desert, but those hopes were now fading fast. I stood poised between excusing myself and leaving, or simply surrendering to my fate. Yet, in Alex, there was also an island of safety and goodwill amidst the dark, brooding energy of the space and the avalanche of words and sensations. So I reached out and grasped the handle of the knife, treating it like a museum piece and laying it across my left palm. Alex never took his eyes off me.

"What's this?" I asked, pointing out the dark green gemstone on the handle.

"I have no idea," he responded, casting my question aside like a scrap of unwanted paper. He leaned forward over the table, his eyes intense.

"Were you ever initiated?" he asked. The question caught me unprepared as I noted the nearest exit.

"How do you mean?" I asked.

Alex considered his response. His voice had quieted down and become slower.

"Well, let me put it this way. I would cut myself with that in front of you and instruct you to do the same if you were my son. You know what I'm talking about? That knife you are holding is for rituals."

I lost the power of speech. Alex saw my discomfort and, like a deer reacting to danger, he changed direction.

"Let's go outside," he said, standing up and walking toward the door. I was still at the table, gathering myself, when Alex's head popped back inside. "And bring the knife!" he called out to me.

I was back outside in the bright light of the Tabernas desert. The washed-out, hazy blue sky had just enough cloud to take the bite off its heat. It was the part of the day when the sun had settled at its highest point, and you braced yourself for some hours of heat.

"Come on, give me a hand," Alex called to me. He was standing at a wooden table with something lying across it. I walked over with the knife and saw a young goat, dead and splayed between us. It was resting on its side, its legs frozen as if it was going to leap from a rock. Blood was pooling under its neck.

"All right, you see that? You're the assistant." He waved his hand over the line of bowls, clothes, knives, and plastic bags in front of me. The cup of tea and chat faded further into the distance. I now had a part to play in dismembering a goat. I stood submissively across from Alex, at the total whim of his instructions. I didn't want to show weakness or let on that any of this was difficult for me.

The dismemberment began. Alex knew what he was doing; his hands and the knife flickered about in front of me. Bags and bowls filled with different types of offal and organs. He bent down low, staring inside the carcass and running his fingers along the ribcage as he casted pieces of flesh to one side.

"Keep scraping the table clean, There's a bucket there," Alex instructed, suddenly all businesslike and serious. He handed me a blunt butcher's knife with a scabbard wrapped in black tape. I used it to clean up the scraps. That became my job. Paul cut and sliced, waved the knife at flies, and cut again, while I kept the workspace clean. He teased away the skin from the different limbs, pulling it loose, then moving on to another piece.

We didn't talk much for a while. Then, finally, Alex looked up from his work. "You're doing fine," he said, wiping sweat from his brow.

And that was how I spent the day.

"Hand me the saw," Alex called out. The muscle in his arm contracted, and the sound of the blade hitting bone filled the air. I winced and closed my eyes. When I looked again, the goat's head was lying in a metal bowl, staring up into the sky.

Alex stood to his full height and rubbed his hands down his sides.

"Okay, here we go. Hand me the ceremonial knife."

The knife had been waiting at the side of the table. I picked it up, placed it in Alex's blood-stained hand, and watched him lift one half of the goat's torso. He held it open with the back of his hand and his lower arm and peered inside, his eyes serious and focused. Time seemed to slow as the knife hovered, delicately held in one hand, the tip pointing toward its destination. It entered, and I dared not move or make a sound. I steadied my breath. Alex's focus was entirely absorbed in the task; his breath was a whisper.

"We are each going to eat a little," he said quietly. "This is a show of respect for the goat's life; we have to mark its passing. A small ritual between two men," he added after a pause. "That okay?"

I nodded, knowing that I was beyond any other response by now. We were two men with blood on our hands, so I awaited my fate.

When the blade was revealed again, the goat's heart lay across it. Alex cut off a few thin slices and held one toward me on the blade. I had lost all autonomy and was now following instructions without question. But I was saved, in a sense. The dogs exploded into life behind us, and I turned to see a stout man entering the compound. He carried another animal's skin in his hand.

"Oh God," I thought. But he walked straight to the table, and his soft tone and smile settled me.

"Paul! Just in time, we're tasting the heart. Want to try?"

"Not a chance," Paul responded without hesitation. I was stunned. The sureness in his voice was a revelation. It elevated him to some kind of hero. I had none of that composure inside me, and in that moment, I longed to access it.

The two men examined the goat skin, assessing its suitability for a drum, when Alex said,

"Well, Paul, this young man is visiting the community around here. Care to show him your place?"

"Sure," Paul responded.

Alex cast the knife to the side of the table, and all the seriousness of the moment faded away. But I still had a piece of goat heart in my hand. I was anxious that Alex would notice. He was chewing on his and chatting with Paul when he suddenly swung around to face me and offered his hand.

"This is a good young man," he said and waved me away.

Paul and I walked back into the desert. The silence felt heavier now, as if the weight of the ritual still lingered in the air. My hand, still warm from the knife's handle, felt like it belonged to someone else. I glanced over at Paul, who was walking ahead, his pace steady, his expression unreadable. He moved with the certainty of someone who long accepted the ways of this land. There was a silence between us that I appreciated after Alex's incessant chatter.

I looked closer. Paul somehow reminded me of a badger. He was stout and close to the ground, with a head of grey hair that just touched his ears. He moved unhurriedly, hands in his pockets, his eyes scanning the terrain and sky. I sensed Paul would prefer silence, but my presence seemed to coax words from him; he muttered at times, and I couldn't always tell if his words were for me or himself. Over time, I realized he was an amateur expert in desert ecology. As we walked, the landscape around us came into sharper focus.

"This is the land of heroic survivors," he said suddenly. "You don't last long here if you aren't tough." He stopped and took a broad stance, pausing as if to share some wisdom he felt I should know. "Some plants grow fast and set seed before the drought kills them; others grow ferociously slow. Thyme steals water from other roots, and Anarbasis articulata—a plant with little ruby-red flowers—photosynthesizes at night." He let that sink in. I felt a wave of disappointment at myself, wondering why everything here had looked like drab rock and dust to me, while for Paul, it was a source of endless fascination.

We sidestepped ant mounds and watched lines of workers heading out and returning. Paul bent down, pulled sprigs of wild thyme, and tucked them into his pocket, then picked leaves from another bush. "Artemisia," he said. I tried to look through his eyes rather than my own, seeing the world as he did.

"This land doesn't hold water," Paul observed, his tone slow and steady. I glanced around. The earth was baked dry, and the rain channels left shadows over scattered wildflowers. "Floods rush through but never get absorbed. You see all these exposed banks? They're carved clean." He smiled at his own turn of phrase.

"Do you have your own house and land?" he asked.

"No," I responded.

"Well, you should. Every man needs that."

"You didn't have to eat that goat heart, you know," he added, pausing to face me on the path.

The last of the meat still lingered in my mouth, and my discomfort must show. "Spit it out," Paul said, turning and walking on.

The sun's heat whistled in the air, a low, searing pitch. The desert is otherwise quiet, apart from the occasional eagle's call and the rumble of distant rockfall. Paul grumbled, muttering names and grievances through his London accent as if talking to the ground itself. He drifted between distant thoughts and the present, sharing his knowledge with me and checking in occasionally. I asked about his house.

"I built it myself, almost entirely on my own, with little help or machinery. Made it invisible. Don't want them to see it." He glanced at the sky and nodded. "Satellites, you know, watching everything."

After a short silence, Paul stopped. "Well, can you see it?"

"See what?" I asked, confused.

"Look again," he said.

I couldn't see anything but dry earth and ravines where rivers once flowed. "Look," he said, working a thumb over the palm of his hand, spitting into the soil, and shaping it into a paste. "Clay. It's everywhere here. That's what I built with. Look closer."

Ahead of us, something seemed almost out of place—a mound of earth, slightly rounded. "You mean that?" I asked, pointing.

"Yes, that," he replied.

I was stunned. His home was nearly invisible, blending into the landscape as if it's part of it. Whatever was beneath that mound, no passing satellite would be the wiser.

"How long did it take you?" I asked.

"Years," he said. "I'm still finishing it. Come on, I'll show you inside."

Paul led me along a low perimeter wall lined with tiny succulents to a wooden door, bolted with three separate locks. As the door closed behind us, the silence of the outside world fell away, and I felt the weight of stone above us. Light filtered in through glass blocks in the roof, casting shafts of color against the sandy walls.

"I found those in a dump," Paul told me, guiding me through a narrow passage with smooth clay walls. We reached a small kitchen, everything the color of sand. A mosaic of a woman pouring water lay at our feet, smudged with dirt and boot prints.

"So, you've come to Tabernas to find a piece of land?" Paul asked, preparing tea.

"No," I say, "I'm just visiting."

"You should consider it. I don't need much here, don't need to go anywhere." He smiled that curious smile. The truth is, I don't know why I've come to the desert or what I'm seeking. But sometimes, the journey brings the questions—and maybe even an answer.

"What do you do?" I asked, deflecting the attention.

"I paint," he said. "Garden, walk the hills, sometimes drink too much," he laughed, "depends how often I see my friend Falko." He handed me a cup of tea and met my gaze. "Do you paint?" he asked, almost challenging me.

"No," I said.

"Well, pick up a craft. A man needs that."

He stood, thinking, then looked at me. "Come on, I want to show you something." We headed back down the narrow passage to a blue door made from wood strips. As he opened it, clay dust fell, and we stepped inside his studio, the air thick with suspended dust. Shelves held small statues, trinkets, and candles, their wax dripping over the edges. A Virgin Mary statue teetered, draped in dust.

"This is where you'll find me," he said. Paul walked directly to a painting canvas in the center of the room. He pulled off a sheet and let it fall to the ground. "I had to paint flowers I remembered from home, from the UK," he said. A painting of brightly painted flowers circled with a crown of leaves was revealed. It stood out in the room, almost victorious, like spring overcoming a long, hard winter.

"Do you go home much?" I asked.

He grimaced. "No. There's nothing there for me."

Paul finished what he was doing and turned to me. "You know," he said, as much to me as to himself, "I am going to the UK this summer to bring that painting to my daughter. She's getting married. She's the only one I'd travel home for."

We spent a short time in Paul's studio, his inner sanctum. He moved through canvases, muttering to himself, while we sip tea and talk of home.

"You're lucky, you know?" he said. "Few visitors ever see my studio. Not even Falko." He grinned, the idea just occurring to him. "Let's visit Falko, anyway, I need a drink!"

He locked the studio behind us, and we stepped back into the searing desert heat. Paul's scarf draped over his grey hair like that of a desert pilgrim, oblivious to the heat. We walked toward the mountains. "I should warn you about Falko," he called over his shoulder. "He's, well, a little mad," he laughed.

It was a short walk, on ground as flat as sieved sand, and before long, a wooden cabin came into view. A man stood in the open ground with a brown horse beside him. He saw us and started waving his sun hat in the air, calling out with a hoarse roar tinged with laughter in the hot, seething air.

"Ooolala, Paul, I'm happy to see you. I can't do it anymore; that damn horse won't move."

He turned to the poor animal, its head hanging low in a look of unruly disinterest. There was a rusted plough attached to it, its metal parts resting lifelessly against the hard soil. Falko looked at the horse as though he was disappointed in every expectation.

"I give up! I can't get the idiot to do the last part." His battered hat was back on his head, comically misplaced, as if barely his. He fished a packet of cigarettes from his breast pocket and shook one out. In one movement, he swung toward me, took both my hands in his and pressed them, then turned to the horse and screamed, throwing his hands in the air again. The horse was going nowhere. "Paul, please do something."

Falko's face and legs were baked dark brown, as if he'd just stepped out of the Australian outback. His accent placed him as Dutch, and he mixed English, Spanish, and his own language in random outbursts.

Paul stepped in to help. He took the rope, held it close to the horse's chin, and tugged once. The horse let out a low groan. He pulled again, more gently, pat its neck with his other hand, and whispered into its ear.

"Ah, Paul, sí, do your magic!" Falko said.

The horse swayed its head a few times and stepped forward. Falko sprung to life, grabbed the handles of the plough, and rocked it into position. "Wait, Falko, wait, have patience," Paul urges, but Falko was already rocking back and forth on his feet, willing the horse to move. Eventually, it did, taking one slow, aching step forward. "Fantástico, Paul!" Falko screamed. The plough began cutting the last stretch of ground, the last arc of the circle.

They worked together: Falko roaring and howling, Paul quiet at the front, whispering to the horse, letting any tension drop from the rope around its neck, and allowing the horse to choose the pace. They reached the end of the line, and Falko exploded in celebration, dropping the plough handles to the ground and giving Paul a great hug and a slap on the back. He hugged me as well, though I'd only stood aside and watched.

"Venga! Let's have a drink," he announced.

He led us to the side of his cabin. Something was brewing outside. Three demi-johns were propped up on a wooden bench in the shade, and one had a tap. He took three glasses from a tray, opened a small plastic chest containing ice, and let a few cubes fall inside each glass. "I don't live without ice," Falko said. Absorbed in this ritual, he crouched over the glasses. "Paul," he said, "I have a good feeling about this year's harvest." He filled them, then reached out to a potted plant, plucked three tiny purple flowers, and dropped one into each glass. With each passing moment, I was losing the desire to drink this concoction, but then, with a smile that no heart could disappoint, Falko swirled around and handed us our glasses.

"To a successful harvest!" he said. It was early afternoon, and this was clearly not his first drink of the day.

We clinked our glasses and drank. It was stronger than it looked. I felt as if I'd been hit on the head with a lump of wood. My eyes closed reflexively from the shock of fiery alcohol hitting the back of my throat as I tried to steady myself. It sank to my stomach, and I grasped my stool with one hand.

Falko roared with laughter, and Paul took another sip. "Good, eh?" he said to me.

Falko continued talking, incessantly, like a cacophony of morning birds. His voice rose and fell with his thick Dutch accent; some words we caught, while others drifted away ungrasped. Yet there was something endearing about his enthusiasm and acute madness. I struggled to keep up. He was the antithesis of Paul, who spoke slowly and measuredly, choosing his words and letting them ease out, like giving slack to a line.

Falko poured himself and Paul a second drink, and I hid my glass between my knees, willing him not to fill it again. He was in his stride now, talking energetically. "Once a year, I admit myself to a psychiatric unit just to have a rest," he said. "It's great; they feed you; it's comfortable; they give you drugs." Paul made no comment on this. He'd heard it before, and a brief moment later, he confirmed that it was true. I considered my own sanity again and wondered how we might measure it, and to what benchmark.

I asked Falko about the land he was ploughing.

"I'm planting an aloe vera farm," he announced, as if it was an idea to rank with the greatest ever conceived. "I met a beautiful African woman last year. She's a real woman. She's coming here in a few weeks to run the farm. I told her to bring all the women she wanted! I want to fill this place with women." He laughed again. Paul raised his eyebrows and sipped his drink.

"Are you looking to buy land here? Because I know some is for sale," Falko asked.

That question again. I hesitated this time, considering my answer. Falko watched me expectantly.

"He's just visiting," Paul answered.

"Oh," said Falko, looking dejected.

My glass was refilled for a second time, and I worried that I was nearing the point of not being able to walk. Falko's wildness was unsettling. My breath was stuck in my upper chest, and my nerves swam in more alcohol with each passing minute. He was self-declared mad, celebrating the fact, as if it's the sanest way to live out here in the desert. Staying the night didn't feel like a good option, so I began to consider how to say my goodbyes. I felt rudderless in the moment, while Falko darted around the back of the cabin, dragging out books on farming for Paul to look at.

"I need to go now," I heard myself saying.

Falko poured me one last drink and dropped a book in my lap. "Just look at this," he said. Both men were talking about farming and planting aloe vera as I leafed through a book on African agriculture. I had no idea why he gave it to me. The book was old, faded, full of black-and-white photos showing people in fields, and surrounded by ancient farming equipment. Little slips of paper where Falko made notes dot the pages.

"You know what you need to do?" Falko said, pausing to make sure I was listening.

"Let him be," said Paul, picking up on my discomfort and increasing drunkenness, but Falko was undeterred.

"No, Paul, listen," he insisted. "This is good." He turned to me again, face serious, smile gone. He set his drink down, speaking more calmly now, relaxed. "What you need to do is hire a horse for three days and take the trip over the Sierra Alhamillas to Cabo de Gato. But before you go, you should eat some peyote, the sacred cactus. Then you'll see there is only one hero in your life, and that's yourself."

Both men looked at me, glasses of their strange blue drink in hand, the smell of alcohol thick in the air.

"Well," said Paul, breaking the silence, "it certainly opened my eyes."

"Yes!" said Falko, "It did, it did! I like to do that trip at least once a year."

They chattered on, and I distracted myself with leafing through the book on my lap. I put my glass of blue liquid aside; neither man noticed, and transferred to sipping from my water bottle. There were offers to stay for food, to stay the night, to join the farm enterprise and work with Falko for possibly the rest of my life, but I eventually stood up and announced that I needed to start walking back to town.

The men walked me out into the open ground. Falko placed both hands on my shoulders, turned me 180 degrees, and pointed into the distance. "Do you see that distant peak? Just walk toward that." And, he said, looking me in the eye again, "If you ever want to hire a horse and make that trip, I know the man to ask!"

I said my goodbyes and departed. I was alone again with the sounds of the desert. Alone with my own thoughts, with the rush of memories of the day that had just passed—of carving up a goat with Alex, visiting Paul's hidden home, and shackling myself to Falko's deranged mind for an hour.

I stepped into the shade of a ravine; the harshness of the day began to soften, and a new kind of understanding stirred within me. The desert, with all its starkness, its cruelty, and its beauty, had carved something into me, though I couldn't yet name it. I felt the echo of these men's presence—their unfiltered, wild spirit—and wondered what steps would lead me to this level of freedom?

The silence of the landscape itself seemed to offer all the answers I needed. The recognition that what just happened was not something that needed to be explained. As I walked, I realized this desert would stay with me. The experience, the blood, the knife, the art and the crazy dreams—it's all still there, lingering in the air around me.

WHERE THE FIRES LEAD

Los Molinos de Rio Aguas, Almeria, Spain

INDALOMANIA, CC BY-SA 3.0 'Rio de Aguas' via Wikimedia Commons

By the end of this tale, I'll be sitting on a boat to Clare Island, seeking some kind of resolution to everything that's happened. But right now, I'm in the south of Spain, sitting with my friends.

"Which is better? To love your home so strongly that you never want to leave, or to travel, knowing you'll never truly belong anywhere?" I ask the group.

We're outside Bar Sol, sipping cold beers under the relentless Almerian sun. The heat pressed down like a lid, baking the streets and rising from the earth like smoke from embers. It felt like fire's omnipresent here, licking at the edges of our thoughts. Without hesitation, Dave responded, "I always travel, but I also go home."

"I had to leave my country. There was no work for me in the Czech Republic anyway," Kris added, flipping a bottle cap onto the table like a spark leaping free.

A truck screeched on the road beside us, and we all instinctively turned our heads. The heat and the sound were jarring, a reminder that things burn, things move.

"So, why are you going?" Kris asked, a mischievous gleam in his eye. "I was just getting to know you!"

"Yeah, Irish, why are you going home?" echoed Jasper, leaning back in his chair, his laughter igniting the group.

I didn't have an easy answer. It felt as though the framework for making this decision had crumbled beneath me. There was nothing solid to rely on, no guiding principle to anchor me. I was adrift in unfamiliar waters, navigating territory that was both unknown and deeply unsettling. It scared me.

What happened next felt like a magnificent cosmic joke. Someone, someplace, was having a fantastic laugh at this. Ultimately, the decision was made for me, and central to it all was the element of fire.

We continued sipping our beers—one of many with these friends—but this one, being the last, was imbued with extra significance.

"Well, come back after August," Dave said. "It's crazy hot till then!" He slaps me on the shoulder, and the others laugh.

Every minute was precious. I looked at an elderly man waiting at the bus stop on the other side of the road. He was sweating under his brown suit and leaning into his right foot, his eyes locked on the road. He looked as many do in these rural parts of Almeria: dressed with unfussy respectability, tough, and short in stature. You see them leaning across the counters of the local bars, sipping cognac, and conversing with other men. I wondered to myself if he had ever traveled.

Kris swung my backpack onto his shoulder. "Time to go."

We finished our beers, return the glasses to the table, and shared quick embraces as the bus pulls up. The next moments blurred: stepping onto the bus, handing the driver money, and finding a window seat. Outside, my friends waved until the bus turns the corner, and then it's just me, alone with the view of Almería slipping away.

I leaned my chin on my hand, the rows of olive trees outside blurring in time with the engine's hum, their perfect rhythm lulling me into a half-sleep. I was leaving. It was decided. Yet, it didn't feel real.

Everything was in motion—the scenery outside, the bus beneath me, and my life on its uncertain course forward. I sat still, letting the rhythm of the engine and the flickering olive trees carry me into quiet reflection. A sadness welled up, mingling with the soft tears I let fall.

My phone pinged. But I ignored it, reluctant to break the fragile stillness. Moments later, it pinged again, and this time, something urged me to look. With a sigh, I pulled it from my pocket, opened the message, and froze.

The words hit like a spark in dry tinder: Due to an incident involving a fire, your scheduled departure has been cancelled.

In an instant, the sadness was replaced by something electric. A fire—a literal fire—had changed everything. Somewhere far to the north, its ripple effect had reached me, pulling me out of my set course like a hand steering the wheel.

The desert continued flashing by outside, indifferent to my elation. We were in the middle of nowhere, a stretch of road where nobody gets off. Nobody but me.

I ignored the signs requesting all passengers to remain seated and walked to the front of the bus. I spoke fast and in broken Spanish, all apologetic and desperate. He repeated my request several times: So, you want to get off? Yes, I told him, right here, in the middle of the road between two towns. He slowed down, pulled over, and opened the doors. A light breeze and warm air came through the open door, and I stepped back down into the arid desert.

I gave up the air-conditioned bus for a battered old car with a half-drunk driver who'd waved me over outside Las Catarinas. By the time we pulled up to Bar Sol, where my friends were still sitting outside, it felt oddly fitting. My first attempt to leave Spain had failed. I rejoined them as though I'd never left at all.

In the weeks that followed, my thoughts often drifted back to childhood—a time when fire held a dangerous fascination for me. It began around age nine, before I understood the concept of safety. I'd steal matches and ignite tissues, tossing them into gardens around our estate, returning later to inspect the smoldering remains. My friend Conor and I once brought a jerry can of gasoline to an abandoned factory, lighting a ring of fire and sliding debris into the flames from the rafters high above. Another time, bored by the river Liffey, I flicked a match into the dry grass and watched in awe as it caught. The villagers ran to stamp out the flames, a chaotic dance that seemed like some medieval ritual. In those days, fire was a game to us, something wild and thrilling. But the risks caught up with me, and eventually, I stopped lighting them altogether.

In the valley of Los Molinos, those memories were on my mind as I walked the short distance down to the valley floor to bathe in the river. Six weeks had passed since my first attempt at leaving, and thoughts of departure were on my mind again. In four days, I was due to leave again, but this time by plane.

Instinctively, I found myself drawn to the river during those weeks. The Rio de Aguas still flows, though faintly—a trickle weaving its way through the undergrowth, where its music once carried to the farms on the terraces high above. In places where the water pools deep enough to slip into, I float on the surface, eyes open, gazing at the abandoned farmhouses clinging to the slope above. Heat, drought, and the relentless desert are dismantling them piece by piece; the last wooden roof beams have already collapsed into rubble. As I lie in the water, I brace myself for these final days in the valley, for the ever-rising heat. And yet, the feeling lingers: This isn't my decision to make.

After enjoying the water, I headed back to the house. On the sunny terrace, everyone was gathered, soaking in the late Saturday morning. The seven dogs sprawled in shady corners, occasionally shuffling over to their bowls for water. A pot of coffee and a two-litre bottle of beer sat among us. From the kitchen, the BBC World Service played faintly, blending with the hum of conversation about my going-away party that weekend.

"Well, Irish, how do you feel?" Pablo asked sincerely, sparking a chorus of responses.

"Ahh, he's not going anywhere!" Kris declared.

"You can't leave," Jasper added.

"Why are you even going back to Ireland?" Nila asked, genuinely puzzled. I had no real answer.

The BBC voice cut through the chatter: "Breaking news." Nobody paid attention.

"Iceland," I heard the voice say, catching my ear. Iceland? News from Iceland was rare. Curious, I walked into the house, where the breeze drifted through open windows. A glance at the computer screen stopped me. A volcano was erupting, sending a vast cloud of ash into the sky. I turned up the volume.

"European airspace is closed," the newsreader announced. "Huge disruptions…"

Dave walked in, caught the report, and burst out laughing. "Oh, for heaven's sake!" he exclaimed, doubling over in amusement. Jasper and Kris joined us, bewildered.

"What's going on?" they asked.

"I don't think I'm going home Monday," I replied, gesturing at the screen.

"Holy sh*t, where's that?" Jasper asked.

"Iceland," I said.

Laughter erupted as the absurdity sank in. Dave's cackling filled the room as I checked my airline's website. Sure enough, my flight was cancelled. Once again, a fire—this time from a volcano—halted my return to Ireland. At least this time, I hadn't paid for a bus.

Four weeks later, as Almeria's heat became oppressive and I wondered if I'd ever make it home, my phone rang.

"Hello, Daithi. Are you in Cork? I've got a job for you, if you're interested." It was Peter, a friend back in Ireland.

I raised an eyebrow. "Go on."

"I need you to rebuild a stone chimney in my house in West Cork."

I said yes. This time, there would be no fire to stop me from going home. But there was one waiting for me when I arrived.

I landed in Cork, and within an hour of arriving at work, Mike the carpenter called me from the roof.

"Did you light the stove in the yurt?" he asked, a note of concern in his voice.

"Yeah, an hour ago. Needed to dry the canvas."

"I think it's on fire."

I dropped everything and ran to the yurt. Black smoke billowed from the back, flames devouring the trellis and roof. Neighbors rushed in, buckets in hand, shouting orders. Mike brought over a hose, and we worked fast, dousing the flames. But it was too late—there was no saving it. My temporary home, destroyed.

I'd only been in Ireland for two days, and I had already set my new home on fire.

That was the moment I decided to go to Clare Island, to get away from all of it. To ask for peace.

The boat ride was quiet, the ocean breeze cold against my skin. On the island, I wandered through fields, not sure where I was going, until I found a small, sheltered beach. I sat there alone, listening to the waves and the wind, trying to center myself.

I didn't understand why all this had happened—why the fires seemed to follow me—but I felt it. I needed to let go. I asked for peace, and then, as if on cue, the wind picked up, and I knew my request had been heard.

The fires stopped after that.

THE HEART OF BRIGHTNESS

Mae Hong Song, Thailand

Ken Marshall, CC BY 2.0 'Salween river, Thailand' via Wikimedia Commons

I placed my map on the brown earth before me, tracing my finger along the river until it came to rest on the village of Bae Mae Son in far northwest Thailand. This was the place where the Andaman Sea absorbs the mouth of the Salween River—a scene I knew I wanted to see. After a month in the south, saturated with comforts and worn by the constant presence of tourists, I longed for something different. Where is Thailand? I asked myself. So I made a plan and headed north.

As one of the few rivers in Asia that remains largely undammed, flowing freely from source to sea, I visualised the Salween on the journey. I saw her beginnings on the Tibetan plateau, cascading over steep canyons, flowing through remote mountains of China and Burma, and finally, in its later course, following the northern border of Thailand and emptying into the Andaman Sea.

I stood out. As a 6'2" Irish man with his knees stretching beyond the handlebars of my moped and an undersized helmet perched like a watermelon on his head, I was a novelty and could not have been happier.

The journey began on a mountain road winding through towering pine, teak, and Asian redwoods. I passed rice paddies with mounds of smouldering straw, the smoke rising like funeral piers. Village names flashed by and I pulled in at a roadside restaurant. The owner looked at me with curiousity and smiled. There was no menu, only what the family was eating that day, so his wife brought me a bowl of vegetable and pork stew. All the food choices of the south had been reduced to this one bowl, and I knew I had arrived. It steamed into my face as I ate. 'Ban Mae Song' the owner kept saying, as though singing, and 'Salween' as these were the only words we both shared.

Do we ever truly know what a day will bring? By the end of this one, I would learn that life is the child outside waiting for us to drop our plans. I would learn other things too. I got lost, missing the turn for the Salween. Smooth tarmacadam got replaced by tracks of gravel, wide vistas by thick undergrowth. I pulled by dust strewn bike to a stop and lay my face on my hands, exhausted and desperate.

A sweet scent brought me back from that place. I raised my head and was looking at a girl. She wore a long black dress with rows of red beads hanging from her neck. Her expression was calm and clear. The aroma, I would learn later, was an incense drifting up from her tribal village and carried by the breeze. She watched me; I said the word Salween, and it hung like a question between us. Then she smiled, seeing me in my desperate state and finding it amusing, she turned to look over her right shoulder and pointed further down the track.

I knew that this part of Thailand was populated by tribal people, some open to visitors, others not. I had no choice. I left the bike where it was and entered the forest. I followed a pathway cleared between the trees. With each step I felt I was moving further away from the world I knew. I let myself be taken away. The friendliness of the tribal girl gave me hope and soon, when the undergrowth turned to open grass, I arrived at the edges of her village.

I stood and looked. On the balcony closest to me, a mother sat. Her child lay across her arms, reaching its tiny head around to get a better look at the strange thing that just emerged from the trees. She looked at me with a detached acceptance, her feet hanging over the balcony, hiding nothing from the world. An elderly man, squatting below, was working reeds into a basket. He thumped them with a wooden mallet.

The village was tiny, and enclosed by steep cliffs with a river running through it. A lost world, a world entirely of itself. I walked on and a young man stepped forward. As though he was my appointed guide he stayed by my side now and led me through the village. On either side, perched on wooden poles several metres off the ground, were their huts. Built of dark wood, the colour of burnt umber, and stained with wood smoke. The roofs were made of reeds, a dark, oily green, reaching down close to the ground and tied in place with long, course rope. Villagers looked down as we passed but no words were exchanged.

I felt like a bird that had wandered off its migratory course. And yet the thought of staying here passed through my mind. Who would I become if I did? The scent I had experienced hung in the air, and it had this calming, almost dream inducing effect on me. I felt at peace and outside of time.

We crossed a wooden bridge where children played at the river's edge. They called out to us, taking turns to lie down in the shallow water. My guide beckoned me on. We left the sound of their laughter behind and walked beyond the village into open fields. Again, I felt myself drifting further from my own identity. How far can we disappear from our known lives, I wondered to myself?

Having no other necessity, I let myself be led. No words passed between us, but a silent understanding took their place. I knew instinctively where he was taking me. I knew this stream was connected to the Salween. We walked like pilgrims across wooden planks that snaked over the wet fields beneath us. Villagers stood up from their work and looked our way. I called out to my guide 'Salween' and he glanced back at me and smiled. He stopped and pointed into the distance. Ahead of us, just visible, the white waves of the Andaman Sea could be seen.

I had arrived. Standing at the shore, I watched the Salween merge with the Andaman, its final act both quiet and profound. This river had flowed freely, carving its way through mountains, fields, and lives, defying containment, choosing its own path. And here, at its end, it surrendered to the vastness.

I thought of my own journey—of plans made and plans abandoned, of roads missed and paths found. Perhaps I had not found the Thailand I had imagined, but something far better: a place that showed me how to let go. The breeze carried the incense of the village to me once more, and I turned to see my guide standing silently behind, his face calm and knowing. For the first time, I noticed the Salween in his eyes, in the stillness of his being.

As the tide rose, I let myself drift one last time—not away from my known life, but deeper into its currents.

THE GOLDEN AGE

Arambol, Goa, India

© Vyacheslav Argenberg 'Arambol Beach' via Wikimedia Commons

The waves of the Indian Ocean lap onto the shore at Arambol beach, a constant presence in the ever-changing evolution of this popular location.

This morning, I am waiting for a man named Guru outside Sri Baba's convenience store. I need to rent a moped for two months, so I've come prepared with money, proof of address, and my passport, bracing myself for a lengthy negotiation.

Guru arrives on a bright orange moped, dismounts with visible disinterest, and sets down a plastic shopping bag of vegetables. With his chin lowered and his eyes wandering, he surveys the passing crowd with casual attention. He's perfectly bald, dressed in a faded purple shirt. Finally, he glances my way.

"Three thousand rupees a month. Call me when you want to return it."

"Where will I find you?" I ask, taken aback by his aloof pragmatism.

He flaps his hand over his shoulder as if shooing away a fly. "Over there."

He scribbles his number on a scrap of paper, gets back on his bike and rides away, the vegetable bag wedged between his feet as he disappears into the crowd.

I am just another tourist in Guru's world. A transitory face passing through. Why am I here? I ask myself, looking into the stream of passing mopeds. Why are any of us here? As if on cue an old hippie appears, a relic of the past, walking in long leisurely strides on the other side of the road. I want to take him by the arm and ask him if he was here from the beginning. In that golden age they speak of when the first travellers arrived. A time when there was no authorities and abundant freedom. But I don't ask. Instead, I watch him be subsumed by the crowd, into the multiple layers of change that Arambol has seen over the years. I make peace with my uncertainty for now and turn the key on the engine.

It is late morning and time to eat. I step into a restaurant off the main road. The menu is lying across a plastic table spread and I flick it open. It is a testament to life here today. There are rows of options for nine different cuisines. I can choose an Isreali, Greek, Italian, English or Indian breakfast and yet, somehow, they all taste the same. The waiter is a young Indian man, thin and neatly dressed in clean shorts and a white shirt. I order a Greek breakfast and ask if he is from Arambol. He finds this hilarious for reasons I can't fathom. 'No,' he says. 'I come from Tamil Nadu,' and walks away smiling.

Tamil Nadu, the The Land of the Tamils, is in the far south of India. Goa is further north, and Arambol is in the northern end of Goa state straddling the ocean. Not long ago, Arambol was part of a remote area with empty beaches and small fishing villages. Fishermen launched their boats in dawn's silence; a single bus ran to town in the morning and back in the evening. Today, Arambol is awash with posters advertising therapists and hypnotists, shamanic breathwork, Tantra circles, and Ayurvedic massage. The fabled Hippie Trail of the 1960's and 70's found its final landing place here, and that influence still echoes through the place.

From the outset, Arambol has carved a 'spiritual' niche, drawing in 'new age' travelers, seekers, and fans of a free-spirited, bohemian lifestyle. If you're looking for casinos, 5-star hotels, or a seamless ride in an air-conditioned taxi straight from Dabolim airport to a poolside resort, Arambol is not your place. Instead, it is dirt roads and bamboo shacks, simple cinder block restaurants draped in Ganesha cloths, streams of mopeds zipping through—a busy current of life.

The first arrivals were escaping Western culture, seeking immersion, not invasion. This was "the first movement of people in history traveling to be colonized rather than to colonize," according to Rory MacLean in *Magic Bus*, his 2006 book about the Hippie Trail phenomenon. Those were the 'good old days' as a seasoned resident might say. But that was then. Today, you can choose the Arambol experience that you want. In a place that touts itself on spirituality whilst meeting the needs of modern tourism, even the smallest markets and cafés now cater to tastes as foreign as they are familiar. And, like the multiplicity of the Indian pantheon, there is something for everyone to choose.

I finish my food and cross the road to Ali's Hyper Market, dodging mopeds and taxis. Despite the ambitious name, the shop is tiny—small enough that I could touch both walls with my arms outstretched. But here, space is a flexible concept. In Ali's eyes, this is a warehouse, packed wall-to-wall with goods.

Ali himself could be Guru's brother by appearance, but his attitude is worlds apart. He highlights the spectrum of local responses you can experience here. He greets me with a beaming smile, as if I'm an old friend, and quickly closes the distance. The aisle barely fits us both, but Ali busies himself moving boxes. "Incense? Ganesha?" he offers, brandishing elephant-headed idols before me. "Coconut oil? Fresh!" In an instant I've transitioned from a smoke-filled street to the private sanctuary of Ali, rich in the aromas of incense. It's overwhelming but exciting.

Eventually, I make my purchases and step out back outside. I walk up the main street only to find myself among a throng of colorful stalls and shouting vendors. Indian women holding sticks hook t-shirts and bags onto stands, their voices calling out with practiced urgency. The call of commerce is relentless here. The women tend to their stalls with eyes that miss nothing. They see my interest in their t-shirts, and their voices find me.
"Sir, come in!"

I retreat to a chai stall, sitting on a small plastic stool and holding my warm cup in both hands. The women persevere. I try to ignore them and eventually they retreat, except for one woman. She steps closer and smiles like a doting grandmother and holds a t-shirt towards me. She is a master of the silent sales pitch. I leave the chai stall with that t-shirt in my bag.

Arambol can be understood in layers - modern amenities layered on ancient practices, tourists on locals, spiritual seekers on curious visitors, cultures layered upon cultures. The walls are plastered with posters, successive high-seasons layered on top of previous ones.

From a four-story balcony, you can see the entire town and how that also is layered, starting with the ocean, that constant presence. It is warm and gentle, touching a beach that is a broad flat expanse where performers, morning yogis, and corn sellers gather, locals and foreigners living side by side. Beach turns to restaurants and venues, then scrubland with faint or nonexistent paths winding through a residential maze - bright pink and green guesthouses. Finally, the town center, with its blaze of moped horns and fumes mingling with wafting incense smoke.

I return to my bike and take a spin out of town. I pull over for a glass of sugarcane juice. An old man with a sideways baseball cap bends the canes and feeds them into a metal grinder. It crushes the pulp and squeezes out the sweetness. I'm mesmerised and scared by the power of the thing. The small diesel motor is sputtering away, groaning under the pressure of the revolving metal wheels. The old man lets his hands slide desperately close to those wheels. I watch the juice run down his fingers and wait for him to wipe it dry. But he doesn't, it dries there under the baking sun. His hands are also layered, successive coats of congealed sugarcane juice, marking the many stalks he has grinded for people like me.

"Have you lived here all your life?" I ask.

He casts me a look. "Under the same sun always," he replies.

And beside the same ocean, I think, as I stand by the roadside sipping my sugarcane juice.

The man sits on a plastic stool awaiting his next customer. He is a few feet from me but it feels like a far greater distance. But who am I to say what is best for this man? The engine of tourism in Arambol is loud and it is the local community that keeps it running. Is he resentful of the changes he has seen or grateful for the extra customers? Either way, life here runs on the labor of the working poor as they accommodate the needs of Westerners. Your breakfast fruit salad was picked by an elderly woman balancing a basket on her head; your coconut prepared by a man with torn flip-flops and a machete. To not see this, you need to be blind or wilfully unwilling.

Where to next, I ask myself. I decide on the beach and return into the stream of mopeds and leave the man by himself at his stall. I find a quiet place to sit, enjoying the warmth of the sand on my palms, and watch the fishermen. They are still here, pushing their long wooden boats out to sea in the morning to return again in the evening, threading between sunbathers and tourists. In the shade of one of those boats is a man untangling his net, pulling at threads and looking oblivious to the world around him, as though we are all migratory birds on the shore for a brief moment.

An elderly man, dressed all in burgundy, sits on the sand not far from me. He could be American, certainly not Indian, but his skin is sun baked and he looks like the country has long since claimed him for its own. He looks over his right shoulder and catches my eye, his face expressionless. Without planning to, I ask if he has been coming here for long. He looks again, as though seeing me for the first time.

'Since the beginning,' he says.

'Wow, how was it back then?

He considers the question a moment. 'It wasn't so great.'

He places a harmonium on the sand and starts chanting. And I am lulled into a restful state. Sri Ganesha, he sings and the ocean waves accompany him. His voice is the only voice I hear and it is beautiful in its fragile simplicity. Ganesha sharanam. As I close my eyes, I hear the waves—constant, yet always new, as if Arambol itself is breathing in and out, adjusting to each new arrival, each new season.

HIMALAYAN DREAMING
Goa, India

Biswarup Ganguly, CC BY 3.0 'Chai Tea' via Wikimedia Commons

It's a mournful sound as a train's engine winds down with a last, pneumatic sigh, like a fatigued beast exhaling. The metal beneath us is silent, and the dust-covered plants outside my window crackle in the heat. This train on the north coast of Goa is not going anywhere soon.

It is late morning, and whoever wants it could have a full seat to themselves. There is forgiveness in this open space to breathe and move around. I gaze up the aisle toward an Indian family, who has taken this pause to spread out a feast. The smells rouse my own hunger. Styrofoam plates with delicate Indian snacks pass across the aisle, children leaping on seats to pluck bites from the moving feast, much to their mothers' annoyance. The women, stern yet glowing in their bright shawls, nudge them back down. The men sit quietly, staring out at the sun-drenched platform. Amidst them sits a grandmother, wrapped in cloth like a hidden treasure. I must have been staring, because her gaze finds me, and like the hard stare of a religious shrine, I look away.

Three hours of delay have begun, though no information has reached us. The driver has locked himself in the cabin, a black hole from which no information escapes. We are left to the forces beyond our control, and this is too much for some. A tall foreigner in light pants and a blue shirt stands, stepping off the train and tapping firmly at the driver's window. "Hello, excuse me, hello," he calls, and knocks again. The window creaks open a fraction. Several fingers appear, pushing it open further until our driver emerges, blinking into the sunlight. He cranes his neck, looking down the track, then roars, "Sanjay!" before shutting the window.

Enter Sanjay, the ticket checker, who strides toward the foreigner with authority and a determined look, stung by the driver's call. His polished shoes slap against the ground at a rising pace, pencil and notebook at the ready. His zeal for his duty is unsettling.

"Stay on the train, please, sir!" Sanjay bellows, eyeing the driver's window nervously. His tone drains the resolve from the passenger, who steps back without protest.

I'm starving. It's one thing to be late, but another to be kept here with an empty stomach. Across the tracks, there's a shop with snacks. I could cross the twenty meters to the footbridge, but Sanjay is blocking my path. "Please stay in the cabin; it will depart shortly!" he shouts at another passenger peering out the door.

Hunger can drive a person to act, even for dried snacks, so I take a deep breath, summon an image of myself as light and determined, and step outside.

Sanjay whirls around, arms raised, screeching at the sight of me as if he'd sensed my escape attempt. It's strange—almost uncanny. His power to catch out rule-breakers is both absurd and oddly impressive. The immediacy of it all shakes me. But I hold my ground, stomach rumbling, set on reaching the shop. Sanjay's footsteps approach, now more ominous. His notebook is out again, which makes me nervous; it reminds me of detention slips in school.

"I just want to buy some…" I begin, but he cuts me off.

"Stay on the train, please, sir!"

"I haven't had lunch," I say, suddenly feeling like a child. Any will to argue deserts me as I plead with my eyes, not just for myself but for the others, equally trapped.

"They will come with food," he says, looking down the empty track. I don't know who he means. Ignoring him and walking to the footbridge crosses my mind, but I dismiss it quickly. I get back in the carriage, defeated, knowing I've played with power and lost.

"Nice try," a young guy across the aisle says, leaning over and handing me a sesame seed and honey bar. "Have it; I've plenty."

Back in my seat, I spot the colorful snack wrappers hanging from the station shop's window. I strain to see them—Bombay mixes, fresh fruit slices, maybe a cold can of apple juice. I would have bought them all.

At the far end of the carriage, a youngster boards with a metal canister of hot, milky chai. His voice is as sweet as birdsong, and his smile spreads down the aisle. I could almost dance for the scent of tea. He lifts the metal container to the table, asking, "How are you, sir?" "Three cups," I say, risking it since the cups are small. He fills them one by one with the thick, syrupy chai.

More vendors trickle into the carriage. A slender man arrives with a basket of neatly wrapped sandwiches, and I buy two. Before I know it, a woman is offering fried chicken, while another man strains over the seats with cups of nuts dangling from his arms. "OK, enough! I don't need more food!" I laugh, and they wander off, already forgetting me.

I arrange my purchases and chat with the guy across the aisle. "So, what brings you to India?" I ask. He's young, well-dressed, with an expensive laptop bag that hints at a certain lifestyle.

"I'm a cameraman," he says, smiling as I recognize the name of the *BBC Wildlife* series. "I'm traveling up to Kathmandu to meet my crew. We're going to film snow leopards."

Suddenly, I'm no longer confined to the train. My imagination roams the Himalayas, and as we chat and satisfy our hunger, I lean back into my seat, letting daydreams drift over me.

Dreams arrive much like this—like underground streams rising up, pushing through the thin fabric of night to kiss the cheek of day. Big dreams, those that stick with us, come like a luminous guest, filling our hearts with questions and maps all in one.

I recall a dream from Spain, where I met the Dalai Lama. In it, he sat in a wide, ornate chair in his Dharamsala home, gazing at me with soft eyes that sparked my attention. His quarters were filled with Tibetan iconography, tapestries, and mandalas. I remember his words less than the warmth they carried. We stood and walked into a large room where people were gathering, and I found a seat at the very center. As he began speaking and silence descended over the crowd, I awoke.

I awoke in Almeria, Spain, the sun just starting to light the edges of the windows. All was silent, yet the Dalai Lama's presence lingered. I rose, brewed a coffee, and read his life story—his exile, his journey over mountains into India, and his new life in Dharamsala. I discovered we shared a birthday, July 6. My heart leapt when I read he was visiting Ireland that summer to speak for the charity Children of the Crossfire at Limerick University. The tickets were already sold out.

A month before the talk, I returned to Ireland. I kept the days around his visit free, letting the thought linger. The day before his talk, I was shopping in town when Jennie, a former classmate, called my name. "Daithí! You came into Susie's dream last night, and she's really upset—she has to talk to you!"

We walked over to Susie, who was sitting in her car. She hugged me, laughing, "You came into my dream and told me I should open a yoga studio in Galway!" We laughed, and then she said, "Hey, we're going to Limerick tomorrow to hear the Dalai Lama speak. Wanna come?"

So it came to pass. We drove north in the bright afternoon, music playing, one dream linking to another. I reached the venue and asked about a ticket; they had one left. I took a seat at the center of the room, where I had sat in my dream. As the crowd cheered, I looked up to see the Dalai Lama holding the hand of Richard Ford, Children in the Crossfire founder. I was fully present, back in my dream, listening with my whole self.

The train jolts back to life, engine humming as we pull away from the quiet station along the Goan coast. By late afternoon, I'm back at my favorite chai stand in Arambol town, where one more Himalayan encounter awaits.

"Do you like it here in Arambol?" a young man asks from a stool beside me as we both sip chai. "I'm Lama," he says. He lives in Kathmandu but spends six months each year in Arambol, tending his shop of Tibetan mandalas and trinkets to send money home to his family. He shows me pictures of his wife and small son, eyes glistening. "My son is two now," he says, pointing to him. Behind them, snow-capped mountains rise.

Lama invites me to his shop, a tiny temple of red walls and incense, Tibetan mandalas hanging everywhere. "Please, enjoy," he says, smiling as I wander, taking in the art. One mandala catches my eye, and I linger.

"That is the Kalachakra mandala," Lama says.

I decide to buy it. Lama carefully rolls the parchment, showing me the correct way to hang it. "This is the top; see? Black at the bottom—very important."

As I leave, he calls out, "That's the Dalai Lama's favorite mandala, you know?"

THE FOX

'A Closing Story'

Peter Trimming, CC BY-SA 2.0 'Young Fox' via Wikimedia Commons

There was once a fox who was having a particularly bad day. All the leaves had fallen from the trees, and summer was a distant dream. It was the middle of winter, and he was cold and hungry. A wind cut across the field that could split a stone in half, and doubts prowled his mind like a band of hunters trying to pull him down.

'I'm not sure I want to be a fox anymore,' he thought to himself. And again, 'I'm not sure I want to be a fox anymore.'

He walked across the frozen ground with his head hanging low when he saw a light shining in the distance. He walked towards it until he came to a large white farmhouse. It was alone in the countryside, with a neat lawn out front and a stone path dividing it in half. He followed the path to the back of the house, where he saw a little structure with a door that was ajar. He pushed himself inside, stood, and looked into the eyes of another animal.

'What are you?' the fox asked.

'I'm a dog,' the animal responded.

'What are you doing here?'

'I live here,' said the dog.

'You live here?' said the fox, as he looked around the dog's home, with the blankets on the ground, the bowls of water and food, and the walls sheltering the cold wind outside.

'Yes, I live here,' said the dog. 'Isn't it nice? I have my own bed, and my owners keep it clean. Every day they bring me food and put it here in my bowl, and twice a day they bring me for a walk—usually to the river across the fields, but sometimes to the forest too.'

The fox felt a longing rise in his heart, and he asked the dog, 'Can I live here too?' This made the dog very happy. 'Sure,' he said. 'There are enough blankets for both of us.'

The fox noticed something around the dog's neck, and he looked at it with all his curiosity.

'What is that?' he asked.

'This? Oh, that's my collar. It's nothing. I just keep it on. It has my name on it and a number to call if I ever get lost.'

The fox looked around some more and saw something else that caught his eye. There was a rope of metal rings attached to the collar, and it was fastened to a post on the wall. The dog looked at the fox with amusement.

'That's my chain,' he said. 'They put that on so I don't run away, but I don't think it's necessary. I mean, I'm not going anywhere.'

'Ah,' said the fox, 'I see.'

A lick of cold wind was curling its fingers around the edges of the door. The fox thanked the dog, said good night, and slipped back outside, back into the moonlight that cast silver threads of light across the land.

Between Here and There:

On Traveling and Belonging

David Martin, CC BY-SA 2.0 'Late rays of sun on forest track' via Wikimedia Commons

I often think of the landscape of home, and one place in particular always returns to me—a soft, hidden patch of grass alongside the river Rye, a stone's throw from the house I grew up in. I visited that spot throughout my early years, and to this day, at the most unexpected moments, the feeling of being there rises up in me. It's a place that holds me quietly, asking nothing, yet leaving its imprint in ways nowhere else can. That place was the whole world for me.

I've carried Ireland with me everywhere. Across deserts, jungles, and cities, I've found myself reaching for something intangible: a sense of belonging, of rootedness, tied to where I began. But I travel because I'm also drawn to the unknown, to the shifting horizon and the promise of a world that moves differently from the one I know. The act of leaving home isn't a rejection but a conversation—a way of asking questions that only stepping away can answer.

Travel has taught me many things, but perhaps the most important is this: true belonging is rooted in a sense of place. And yet, there's a paradox in travel. The further you go, the more pieces of home you begin to see reflected back. A fragment of a song, the smell of a distant sea, or the way the light falls over a foreign hill—all these things carry echoes of where you've been. And yet, there are moments when you feel untethered, a stranger even to yourself, and it's in these moments that the pull of home is strongest.

In Mae Hong Son, Thailand, I felt belonging in the warmth of strangers who welcomed me into their homes, despite our shared language being only smiles and gestures. In Tabernas, Spain, the harsh desert heat reminded me of Ireland's soft rains, a contrast so stark it brought an ache of longing for the familiar.

Ireland is my constant, the place that gives meaning to all my wandering. It is not only where I began but also the lens through which I see the world. Being Irish has shaped how I interact with other cultures—with curiosity, humor, and a deep respect for all that they share. And yet, stepping away from Ireland has made me see it anew, appreciating its quiet strength and resilience in ways I couldn't while standing on its soil.

Travel, for me, is an act of discovery, not just of new places but of the self I am in those places. It has taught me to embrace the tension between belonging and longing, between the urge to wander and the need to return. I've learned that home is not diminished by travel; it is enriched, just as travel is enriched by the memory of home.

I began this collection with a quote from T.S. Eliot: *"We shall not cease from exploration, and the end of all our exploring will be to arrive where we started and know the place for the first time."* For me, that place will always be Ireland. And the roads that lead away from it will always bring me closer to understanding what it means to belong.

Ireland, with its soft light and open skies, is where I come back to center myself. But the call of the road will always be there, whispering promises of stories untold. And so, I will keep traveling, knowing that each journey will bring me closer to home, no matter how far I wander.

I hope these stories have inspired you. For more reflections, updates, and new adventures, follow me on Substack. Just scan the QR code to stay connected.

https://daithineavyn.substack.com/

The House of Oaks and Owls

Printed in Dunstable, United Kingdom